Become
the
Pebble

Rainmaker Publishing

First published by Rainmaker Publishing 2024

Paperback ISBN: 978-1-961351-14-1
Hardcover ISBN: 978-1-961351-16-5
Author Headshot Image: Leonard Kinsey, LPK Studio
Book Cover Design: DeGuie Sanabria
Publishing support services provided by Rainmaker Publishing. To learn more visit: www.timetogetpublished.com

Become
the
Pebble

Rainmaker Publishing

Los Angeles, California

A Collection of Eclectic Poems

Bonnyeclaire Smith Stewart

PRAISE FOR BECOME THE PEBBLE!

"This thoughtful poetry collection by Stewart is astounding in the depth, variety of themes, and power of personal transformation and freedom that it offers to the reader.

Themes range from personal racial and gender history, the power and beauty of Nature, the influence of southern culture, thwarted dreams and wishes, her search for love and meaning, to obstacles of exclusion, betrayal, despair, prescribed gender roles, and violence as a child and woman. There are also themes of solitude, color politics, single parenting, health and aging.

Stewart questions the uses of technology, the prescribed power of skin tone, various forms of intimidation, and sexual control by others.

The great variety of themes is balanced by themes of freedom to choose (speaking out, independent travel, non-conventional dress and behavior), hope, advice, affirmations, redemption, and personal transcendence.

Stewart is an influencer touching others like the ripples of the pebble she becomes. She uses memory and metaphor, varying poetic styles, imaginative details of intergenerational love and family relationships, veiled numerology, and religion to illustrate her search for metaphysical meaning, happiness, romantic love, and self love.

Finally, Stewart's quest for and personal philosophy of freedom emerge in this book, as she finds her voice to express, in poetry and song, and share her wisdom of escape from traditional expectations to peace, higher love, and restoration.

An excellent and sometimes challenging book!"

~Kathryn Waddell Takara, PhD, Publisher, Author
American Book Award: Pacific Raven Press: Hawai`i Poems

Table of Contents

To God whose creation forms pebbles in an array of colors and textures over extended periods of time up to thousands of years. To my parents and other splendid mortals along my path who helped shape and mold me; like the wind and water, over time, refining rocks and sediment into pebbles. For pebbles, teaching patience and the impact of taking the leap to act and react to life each day.

"Birds sing not because they have answers but because they have songs."
~ African Proverb

"When you choose to take the leap, you awaken and release your greatness."
~Bonnyeclaire Stewart, 2024

"What happened to you yesterday and last week and six years ago and ten minutes ago and what you surmise may happen tomorrow is poetry-in-the-rough. Strain it—still—work the magic of carefully-chosen words upon it—and there's poetry."
~Gwendolyn Brooks on Poetry and the Poet's Life

Foreword

Currently, Bonnyeclaire is a member of a weekly meditation and poetry reflections group that I lead. We first met at Sarah Lawrence College. Our friendship was cemented during the fall of our junior year when we were the only two patients in the college's infirmary. At the end of the day, when the staff had gone home and left us with instructions on whom to call in an emergency, we'd settle in for long late-night conversations. I am white and grew up in the Midwest. Bonnyeclaire is Black and from the South. Her stories drew me into a world I knew nothing about. There was also much laughter. Life with Bonnyeclaire is always full-charge ahead. I've treasured our friendship for more than fifty years. We continue to share our challenges and commitments, and I continue to be filled with admiration—for her abundant courage, her resilience, her sense of humor, and most of all, for her unending giving of herself to something larger.

Bonnyeclaire chose to Be a Pebble at a young age. She's been dropped into deep water numerous times in her life, creating ripples that have opened doors previously closed to African Americans and women, and ripples that affected her personally in both positive and challenging ways. At 16, she attended high school in Connecticut as part of the NYC American Friends Service Committee's "Southern Negro Student Project." With the encouragement of several mentors, she went on to Sarah Lawrence College. As an adult, she has sung professionally and pursued careers in child development and later in business. She launched 4MillionVoices, a nonprofit organization that amplifies African American history through researching, documenting, and publishing accounts of individual lives of African Americans. She also writes poetry, fiction and nonfiction. She was a wife, and is a mother and grandmother. She has survived serious health challenges, always pursuing traditional and alternative treatment modalities. Her connection to Spirit, to God, is deep and ever-present.

It's one thing to Be a Pebble; it's much more when one shares what it feels like to be The Pebble and the ripples you have created. Moving away from analysis, Bonnyeclaire's poetry takes us into the experiences of being a woman, of being a slave, of being alive in this terrifying and wondrous world. Her poetry speaks to my heart. It opens doorways to ways of knowing and understanding experiences in my own life as well as in those of others—of slaves, of Black women, of African Americans. I believe her poetry will draw you in too, and you will be changed by it.

Diana C. Leslie
Wednesday Meditations and Poetry Reflections with Diana
Mystic, Connecticut

Introduction

In this collection of poems, I invite you to delve into the profound wisdom of life's simplest treasures - the pebbles overlooked in our rush through existence. Each verse is a reflection of the lessons gleaned from observing nature's quiet miracles - the raindrop's journey, the delicate petal's bloom, and the patient formation of a pebble. These poems are more than mere words; they are fragments of my journey towards understanding, stitched together with threads of experience and introspection.

Inspired by the notion of becoming the pebble, I embarked on a quest to uncover the significance hidden within the ordinary. Just as a pebble undergoes a transformative journey, so too do we as we navigate life's twists and turns. Through observation, participation, and ultimately immersion, we discover the essence of true existence.

Join me as we embark on this three-phase pebble experience together. From mere observation to active participation, culminating in the brave decision to become the pebble ourselves, each step offers a deeper understanding of our own potential and purpose. Just as every ripple carries the echo of its origin, so too do our actions resonate throughout the tapestry of life.

Beyond the visible surface ripples, when you become the pebble and take the plunge, a new revelation is experienced. You will discover that for every degree you descend into the deep, there is a corresponding ripple. The multiple layers of vibrations transmitting the impact of your actions can have unprecedented outcomes.

"Become the Pebble" is not just a title; it's a call to courage, a testament to the power of embracing our true selves and diving headfirst into the unknown. Through these poems, may you find inspiration to live your bliss, live your passion, live your dream; and become the pebble that creates ripples of change in the world.

LIVING FREE

Sugar Lace

Bodies laced with sugar
        Drenched in fat
        Used to have a waist
        Now, wonder where it's at

Refined sugar
        Refined oil
        Stress out the body
        Causing labored turmoil

Chemicals in the water
        Chemicals in the air
        Chemicals in the soil
        Causing much despair
Chemicals in the food we eat
        Bread aint bread
        Meat ain't meat
        Who wants a GMO treat

Lies on the label
        Lies in the ads
        Mostly all the food we eat
        Is just plain ole bad

Sugar in the body
        Sucre in the brain
        Azucar in the heart
        Adding it ain't too smart

Sugar in the spirit
        Sugar in the soul

Sets a chain reaction
Killing us before we're old

Bodies laced in sugar
Are sickly and sad
Trapped in a system
That's gone greedy mad

Bodies laced in sugar
Walking around on earth
Folks are crying,
Leaving earth dying

.........Bodied in sugar lace

Become, Becoming, Be the Pebble

Popular are "chase your dream" and "find your passion."

Is there a prelude?

After the introspective "follow your bliss," consider "become the pebble."

We have all seen a picture of ripples in the water from a tossed pebble.
What if you were actually standing on the bank of that water?
       Tender grass under bare feet
       Warmth of a brilliant sun
       Blue sky and white clouds over head
       Feathered chirps and melody serenading
       Gentle breezes caressing
       Spotting random pebbles

You casually take a pebble of your choosing,
       And toss it in the water
       You feel
       arm muscles stretch
       the texture as it's released
       You sense
              anticipation
              wonder
       You hear
              plop as it hits the water
       You see
              a single small circle
              magically become many and widening
              seemingly endless ripples from one small pebble
Then again, what if
You stood on that same bank of water

And <u>became</u> the pebble

      Tossing your whole being...body soul spirit...into the water
      As you descend, you realize
      For every degree downward, there is a corresponding ripple
      Endless impact...effect
      From one act of boldness...adventure...giving of one's self

Be infinite...BE the pebble

Only after in becoming the pebble can you
truly live your bliss, live the dream, live the passion!

Break Away

De Rompre.
Qui? Je jois partir!
Who? Me. I must leave -break away! Soon.
I decided I needed to get from the land's interior
To where the exterior meets the fluid gateway
To the horizon.
But it's winter. Will Spring ever come?
I need to break away. Soon.
I think I'll rent a convertible,
Put on white cotton shorts and wear my white and black
Threaded peasant blouse, loosely off shoulders,
Black leather flips, graced by a sterling silver toe ring
(symbolically on the one who was supposed to stay home),
Graced by delicate seashore molds shimmering
On a silver ankle bracelet
Arm bangles, Ear hoops, Iridescent blue circular British shades
For my hazel-browns, reflecting coral painted lips, and smile
Caressed by silver locks, fragranced by Cartier. Bag
In the trunk. Key in ignition. Motorized top
Down ... Full view of an
Endless blue sky, glorious white cloud clusters, brilliant
Blinding sun, Smell of honeysuckle and freshly
cut grass, just after a quick fallen rain flash,
On ramp...Open Road...music, wind, though missing
A special someone to share. Maybe
I'll meet him somewhere out here.
De Rompre – I need to break away!

Choices

Choices have consequences, even in choosing life or death
Attitudes impact choices
Choose to
Live Long
Live Well
Live Happily

There is more to do
The best is yet to come
Live to love
Let love lead attitude and choices

Be quicker to forgive
Be kinder and more helpful
Be slower to anger
Be a better listener
Be easier to love

I Hope You Dance

wear the dress,
take the trip,
buy the shoes,
make the phone call,
drive your dream car,
sing the song (loudly),
love totally,
live like no tomorrow,
and above all-
I hope you dance.

Maybe

Maybe it's garbage
Maybe it's gold
Not sure which, but gotta
Pour out my soul

Been a long time comin'
Too long you might say
Try overcoming a kind of hell
Day after day

You're a girl so it's gender
From the South,
Cancels contender
Ha! You're brown

Means got no ground
And... if you're poor
Don't stick around
Truth be told
Whether young or old
If you lighter than light
Or black as night
In this country you got no place
No kinda assurance, no safe space

Maybe it's garbage
Maybe it's gold
Same old story
Is regrettably old

The It Factor

Some have 'it' hot
Some have 'it' cold and
Some just have 'IT'
Solid 24K gold.
Talent, smarts, beauty, and heart as
Pure as gold.
Not a guarantee to get a fair shot or
Honest start
Playing the game is luck of the draw
Some producers want to gnaw and paw.
Sell your body
Sell your soul
What's the going price to reach your goal?
For her
A price too high to pay fame's cost and
Poof!
There goes her chance, all was lost.

Little Moments

Life is
> a collection of little moments

Notice and
> appreciate as many as you can

Love is
> giving your heart
> without expectation
> in thousands of moments

All we have is
> lots of little moments
> in the now
> to cherish

Let us
> meet the moment
> breathe the moment
> touch the moment
> feel the moment
> live the moment

The Option

Why has no one told us
       Illness is an option?
       What? This sounds absurd.

Hold this thought:
"Humans have logic and reasoning based on experiential learning –
learned by doing – our experiences"
We learn early to make choices.
We have power
We have authority

In truth it's simple

   Stress interrupts the natural state of being at rest – in a state of "ease"
       Stress starts a fight or flight series of events
           Triggering cortisol
           Then adrenaline
           Which has a ripple effect throughout the body
       Shifting from a state of "ease" to a state of "dis-ease"
       Prolonged imbalance of dis-ease causes malfunctions, aka illness

The power, the authority, the victory is how we choose to respond to
stress
Choose to avoid stressors; and when that is not possible de-escalate,
ASAP
       That's the option. To choose or not to choose,
       That _is_ the option
      that is _the_ option
      that is the _option_
that is the option!

Certainty

Certainty has its place
But not always appropriate
Sometimes downright 'b o r i n g'

On the other hand

Uncertainty has its place
to rock the boat
urge change
may be scary but
Never 'b o r i n g.'

~~White~~ Light Privilege

Oh no! Did she just say that?
Did she just say "how white of you?"
Damn. Never in a thousand years did
I think she would let her brown skin
Be a weapon against my light skin
The legacy of slavery haunts us still
To use the enslavers weapons, at will
How deep goes the dagger,
How painful the words
Hard to erase the hurts
They sting in your memory
Emotional smoke ascends your chimney
These words you can't take back
The friendship singed
Totally unhinged
Are days of light privilege gone
From Master's divide on skin tone?
Where light skinned worked in the big house
With breached endogamy of a spouse
And got ivy admissions in the sixties
And jobs in the seventies
And raises in the eighties
And luxuries in the nineties
And openly married white
Somehow light privilege is still a plight
Even though it's not alright

Heroes

We seem to need heroes
Why?
Why do we need heroes?
The need to build high and higher pedestals
Humans cheered, and loved, and addicted
by fans
creating idols
then we are seemingly crushed when
heroic feet of clay reveal
human frailty
reduced to ordinary status
after which
there can be mourning the heroic loss, or
discarding, or even crushing, and
destroying, when the evitable has occurred.
In the process, they are reduced to ordinary status
like the rest of us.
Can we not find inspiration within ourselves?
Are we not *all* heroes?
Don't ordinary people do extra-ordinary things every day?
Look at me—Look at you—Look at us and
See a hero!

Digital Witness

Living in the age of the Digital Witness
Can inspire creative ways to achieve privacy
Got tape on computer camera
Techy people do it, so it's good enough for me
Is Big Brother really watching?
Is the digital witness monitoring, even
When I'm surfing in my bra?

Cell phone locator
Smart watch apps
Two-way cameras?
Satellites, drones
Cell towers and 5G
Who *is* the digital witness?

iCloud, cyberspace, super highway
Open us to the global stage
While also home to Identity thieves, thieving
Phishers, phishing
Onlooker
Watcher
Looker-on
Listener
Eye witness
Ear witness
Digital witness

Color

Color is a descriptive word.
The color of my skin was never intended to define who I am.
That's it. 'Nuff said.

The End.

Present

Being present is a wonder.
Most people look but do not see!
They do not see what is before them
Or anything in between.
Many people hear but do not listen
They are preoccupied with their
Own egos and agendas.
Often, they simply wait for a pause
To speak; however when
They open their mouths to
Speak, words flow outward but hardly
Have real meaning for the listener.
Presence is sacred. Being present is
A responsibility we must acquire
For our own benefit and profitable for
All within one's realm. Being present
Is an aid beyond communication exchanges.
It allows treasures to unfold...when
You seek, you will find; rather than
Aimlessly seeking; and wandering
With no reward.
The presence of one who is present
Is something we all desire and deserve.

Thrones of Flesh and Bone

Some of it, I heard

Some of it, I read

Some of it, I lived

is it not enough to live in a country

where you remain at the bottom? Where

myths, stigmas, and the 100-plus derogatory slang

words outnumber any other race or religious group? Where

educational, housing, political, religious, economic, employment, cultural,

and medical prejudices are prevalent in the forefront and recesses of minds – and

hearts – and documented on papers hidden and seen; existing and destroyed. Reflecting

a methodically designed and maintained in systemic order to keep you stayed? Yet, none of this

cultural torture seems to quench the thirst in a "democracy" where all human beings are created

equal, as "we the people." There is a greater torture than that of race-which may seem to dilute its

effect, effect, effect. Self-identity, self-worth, self-dignity are a daily challenge to maintain- as is success,

Which must be taught to each generation differently than any other group–Both with"in" and with"out"

In and Out..out and in, inward and outward of the veil. Stifling and smothering the 1 drop of Africana

blood-race who, despite suffocation and degradation created systems (plural) of music; engineered

agricultural landscapes; designed GPS, and cell phones, lost countless stolen ideas and patents,

the traffic light, the clothes dryer, vehicle automatic gear-shift; modern toilet, lawn

sprinkler, soul-food cuisine, potato chips, Jack Daniels Bourbon, peanut butter,

eradicating cataracts, open-heart surgery, astronauts from outer space,

and the known list goes on and on and on; not to mention the

countless unknown contributions of those whose DNA

connects to the cradle of mankind, whose past

present and future hinge on those who

sit on thrones of flesh and bone.

Not At All

Promises written in water
are no promises at all

Plans written in smoke
are no plans at all

Words spoken in sunbeams
are no words at all

Support given in clouds
is no support at all

FOR

Promises made in water
never make a mark

Plans written in smoke
only dissipate hope

Words spoken in sunbeams
cannot be grasped

Support given in clouds
disintegrate and float away

Black Snack

Don't wanna 'be' Black
Just want a Black snack

Don't wanna really 'know' us
Think you are above us

No need to bargain or even ask
Take as little or much, without mask

No apology, no explanation
In the American civilization

Chasing the Dream

Having 'a' dream
Having dreams
When do you start having dreams?
How do you decide on a, or the pursuit?
Where do you begin chasing dreams?
Is there a 'the' dream?
Can you have more than one?
How do you choose when, where and how to chase?
Did you realize the dream(s)?
What was the dream?
Was it really a dream?
Did you pursue?
Is there a right dream?
What would happen if you didn't live it?
Did life get in the way?
Were there dream snatchers?
Did they win?
Is it too late?
Maybe.... Maybe not
You decide what dream, and when where and how to
Chase the dream

INNER CHAMBERS

Escucha Me

I know, not only why the caged bird sings, but why the
imprisoned soul must dance.
Living alone – is it a haven of peace, or a four-walled prison?
Feeling pretty fragile these days,
Dreams border-lined, as deferred, and
Wishes melting, like warm caramel on a mound of dark
chocolate.
Rescued from the inside out and outside in.
The bellowing sounds of Gypsy Kings' Best - fills the room.
Chords, musical, with guitar fingering and syncopated drums
Sensually intertwined with chords, vocals, ever sooooo male.
My feet tap, hands reach!
Abandoned castanets agree, and I begin with
Reminiscent red dress flamingo moves.
"Sin Ella" beckons .... commands
Move and be free to the Brazilian heartbeat of joy, love, and life.
Dreams sustained by hope, deeper and deeper
elevate outwardly higher and higher
On notes musical, wider and wider
On drum beats, deeper and deeper
By seven male voices.
Ole!
Baila con me!
Escucha me? (listen to me?)

As it Turned Out

As it turned out, not only was she
a brilliant scholar, she had a heck of a voice that
was clear and resonant, comforting yet provocative.

The kind of singing style that makes you want
to embrace the sublime melancholy
that is love and life and wine on a midwinter's night.

Or in the breeze of a midsummer's eve, and
she was beautifully formed in petite svelte proportions,
hazel-ring brown eyes graced by sun-kissed curls, changed
from brown to hazel, in her mood-twirled world.

When she sang her songs, and owned the stage she
connected with her audience freely like a bird uncaged.
Like the wind in flight, her message had might.

Whether tender or tight -ly knitted in play,
she communicated words and music moving through
and from her soul, body and spirit, as if
she were creating melody and lyric, just for you.

Yet the universe would never hear her sing for
permissions were not granted, from parental taboos and
marital envy. The world will never know the voice it
missed or captivating movements of feet and twists.

Born for the stage, a space she could command, for
the humble, the poor, the proud, the swanky her lungs
would expand, to tell irresistible melodic
tales across cultural barriers in any land.

"Good" – Bye

How do you say "good-bye"?
Why do we say it?
Is there a need?
What does it mean?
...so long for now
...until we meet again
...okay 'til next time
OR ....
This is it!!!!
Don't plan on seein' ya' agin'
Ever
Never
Soooooo, how you say good-bye, depends
On what you mean, and
It helps to make sure the person knows
What you mean when
You say "good-bye"
With words, "I don't think we should see each other anymore."
With hints, "I need space."
With gestures, like the dismissive hand,
With offerings, good-bye dinner, or "dessert"
Say what you mean when you mean to say good-bye.
Can we always find the "good" in good-bye?

Just A_____

She realized she was just an object - girl
  a sexual object
  a repository for his relief
  a meaningless conquest
  a notch - of sorts

She realized she was just a trophy - wife
  a prize
  a show piece
  a victory
  a triumph - of sorts

She realized she was just a piece - of pussy
  a good time
  a sport
  a booty call
  a rendezvous - of sorts

She realized she was a thingy -thing
  a beauty
  a distant admiration
  a misuse
  an abuse - of sorts

She realized she was just a - pacifier
  a conscience easer
  a subconscious pleaser
  a toy teaser
  a pleasure leisure - of sorts

She realized she was just a - curiosity
  a novelty

an oddity
an idiosyncrasy
a peculiarity - of sorts

and yet, not a rarity at all...she realized she was
from time, in memoriam, one of millions of 'just a'

Relationship

A relationship is like a house
Built on a sure foundation or on sinking sand
Use of natural elements or synthetic materials
It is whatever the occupants make it

If you have unresolved issues
They "will" be revealed in a relationship
Respect, trust, commitment, love
Desire to be in it, to win it

Showing the other
They made the right decision
In choosing you – e v e r y d a y

No secrets
Transparency
Letting go
Resolve all before bed

So Simple

It is all so simple.
It is all about love.
The mystery of
The meaning of
Life.

It has always been about love
Love of Creator
Love of Creation
Love of Creatures...human and all other two-foot, four-foot, many
footed

The single most thing the enemy
Tries to destroy early in life is love
Feeling and actually being unloved

The meaning of life is Love
Love one another – regardless
God is love – for He so loved the world
Love your enemies

Love, love, love
Luv, luv, luv

You Are Music

When you speak to me in that special way, It's music to my ears.
When you stand in front of me and look into my eyes, it's music to my eyes.
When you reach for me and embrace me and touch me, it's music to my body.
When you adore me and admire me, it's music to my soul.
When you give yourself to me, it's music to my spirit.

You are all instruments and all voice ranges in perfect harmony
You strum me with your fingers
You caress me with your hands
You stroke me
You tap me
You pluck me
You   me.
Your breath upon my face is a gentle wind instrument,
Your movement in dance to the rhythm of a drum,
Your grasp of my hand initiates internal bell tinkles,
Your body in motion with mine, in syncopation, in all forms
Even when you are asleep, next to me, it is a quiet song
Gentle breathing, head on chest, heart beating
Beckoning me just before first light
Saying my name in baritones, just right
You are music to me!

PURELY

To love purely, from afar, without expectation
One-sided love...is it love, at all?
How long is too long for one-sided love?
Is that the only pure love?

Reciprocated love comes with expectations,
Giving without selfish gain
Having mutual needs met
Nurturing, attentive, unselfish
Other-focused, gives inner satisfactions.

Given purely, has a transformative affect,
A lasting effect. Love for love's sake.
Simply, to love one another.
Purely

Love Goes

How far will love go?
How far will true love go?
To the ends of the earth—or beyond.
Til death do us part—or beyond.
Love goes where it needs to go
as far as it needs to go.
True love is not limited to time, space, person, place or thing
True love knows no boundaries.
Love goes

BETRAYAL

Betrayal, in the moment, discovered,

can   stun
            shock
            anger
            deflate
            defeat

It's a kind of cognitive dissonance
            double truth
            double lie
            truth wrapped in a lie
            lie enveloped in truth

Recollected betrayal in memories is the worst habit
            holding you captive in
            perpetual or
            intermittent
            b e t r a y a l memories need to be released

One that imprisoned me for a season was
            for a few moments in time he
            made me feel special
            ....chosen
            ....wanted
            ....desired
            ....loved
For those moments, I needed to feel all of that. The rude awakening, though painful, began my healing.

Stability

Finally—self achieved inner stability and security
the absence is
unstable
unanchored
unrooted
unbalanced

Feeling	tolerated
Causes	searching for attachment, belonging, wandering in need of stability, security vulnerability to empty words of prey
Wanting	to be rooted anchored in relationship in spaces
Feeling	wanted worthy safe secure stable

Three Gils

I knew three Gils
Who were all special to me
One I knew since birth,
He was my brother, Gil

The next one was a pre-school cutie
Short knee pants in Sunday School
Held my hand and sat on my lap
Later became my brother-in law, Gil

The third, I knew since high school
He was brilliant, and full of compassion
Played keyboards, helped the community
He was my friend, Gil

One by one they left for a better place
I can still see each face
I smile at the memories
In my mind's eye

In my heart's eye

Hmmmmmm

Hmmmmmm,
It's Friday - - - night- - - again. Sigh!
Playing softly in the background is easy, mellow jazz
on YouTube over a static image of a cozy NYC bedroom.
Sitting on my comfy beige leather Italian sofa, and
Penning these thoughts.
Yep! It's Friday night again. And I am alone. Damn.
Too frugal to pay for subscription, so am interrupted, but
Not bothered by commercial interruptions.
Don't get me wrong. Not E V E R Y Friday or Saturday
Causes me to pause.
Is he out there? Like the musical, Oliver? And like
The musical song "Where Is Love?", I asking...
W h e r e I s L o v e for me? Not just any ole
Love. I'm talking fulfilling, committed, respectful
Agape – yep, the unconditional stuff...good
Stuff. When I ponder bees buzzing around the
Hive, it begs for pause.
Guys from long ago, some now married
Who profess deep long-term love over the
Years—not acted on. They say
Because intimidated that I would have rejected
Them—outright. And the other group
Of unmarried men, are either controlling freaks
Or lack courage. I did not realize until recently
That many men are stuck in pains, emotional
Traumas from their past. While others are simply
Caught up in their male chauvinist tendencies.
Where is he? He who I close my heart's eyes to see... H'mmmmmmm

Rush

When I see you
I want to run to you
Like the water rushes when the damn breaks.

When I am with you
We defy gravity
And escape, with a subtle rush, to our personal space

Where there is no time
Or boundaries in that place
Of quiet bursts that gently rush

You suspend me
You bend me
You mend me

You refresh me
You revive me
You rush me

Love, You Say?

Love is a many-splendored thing, OR
Is love a many-splintered thing?
There is no doubt in 1952 author
Han Suyin; and again in 1955 lyricist
Paul Webster expressed the meaning
Of "splendored" love as spectacular.
A love expressed by
Brilliance, gloriousness, gorgeousness,
Grandeur, magnificence, nobleness
Majesty, resplendence, And certainly
– splendidness! Paired with fabled ideal in
Images of princes on white stallions and
White castles. Love is lovely for ever and ever.

But what kind of love do we bring to one
Another? Is it possessive and limiting with
Monitoring and controls? Is it angry with
Slander and violent assaults? Is it distant
And cool, cooler, cold? Is it absent or
Monotonous with worn rhythms, grown
Tiresome and old? Or is it splendid and
Respectful, committed and kind; full of
Passion and relief from the daily grind?

In 1984 Foreigner bellowed "I wanna know
What love is, and I want you to show me."
Surely, he meant what most of us have in
Mind...the splendored thing. Sue Kidd wrote
"every little thing wanna be loved" in 2001.
We know this because LOVE has been written
About since the beginning of time; and that is

Because it is <u>the</u> single most important human need.
Not to be owned or mistreated or splintered. Rather,
To be cherished and adored-loved as splendored!!!!

Sapiophile

The day my friend told me
Her google find revealed a mystery that
Evaded me until that very
Moment in time, when she explained,
In detail, she and I were sapiophiles.
News to me—what in the world
Does it mean? Sounded odd, yet
Intriguing. The short of it is
Sapiophiles find intelligence
Sexy. Recalling as early as five years old
Every crush, and each love has been an
Xtra smart, intelligent, brilliant man
Yes, I'm a sapiophile, are you?

ALMOST

I almost died in the womb
When my twin sister vanished
She whispered, "I can't make it,
You go on."
A vanishing twin is a common phenomenon
The occurrence of which has been recently documented
Through modern technology
As a common occurrence.
A vanishing twin can be reabsorbed into the mother
Absorbed into the twin sibling
Or birthed as a thin papyrus-like collection of cells.
And I, unknowingly, was gifted to live with the
Vanishing Twin Syndrome.

Sugarbaby Love

When the first grandbaby was born—tiny little bundle that she was
Shifted my being the instant I saw her
I was overcome with unspeakable joy
A joy I had never known
And a new classification
No longer an ordinary person
"I" was a bonafide grandmother

Though I did not know exactly what that meant
A sense of it was beginning to unfold
Oh, I'd heard how you get silly in love
And enjoy without responsibility
But in the moment, none of that was present

What was occurring in those first moments was
an inner awareness
The bottom of my heart opened as if
A secret trapdoor was released
It was velvety and luxurious
Deep—No bottom—endless

Overwhelmed, I wept
Silent tears of joy
Looking upwardly thankful
Never conceiving the dimensions of this depth of
Love for the bundle I would call my Sugarbaby
And all the grands to follow would be my very own Sugarbabies!

More than Words

When he looks deeply, staring into my eyes
When he takes my hand in his on the way to the car
When he leaves a smile face on a post it
When he puts his arm over me while sleeping
When he purses his lips to me across a room
When he pulls me close into his space
When he kisses gently and lingers, several minutes
When he warms my tea abandoned by a call
When he rubs my aching shoulders
When he does something without a prompt
When he drives long miles, insisting that I rest
When he offers his chest for my head to nest
When he, shows affection, and respect, and love
       in many ways, more than words

MORE THAN TREES

Fresh

On my way home, windows down.... smell of fresh cut grass

Walking out of the grocery store....smell of fresh summer rain

Stepped into bakery....smell of fresh baked bread

Held my first born....smell of fresh new baby

Bought first bottle....smell of perfume freshly sprayed

Ran the race....smell of fresh sweat

Physical intimacy...fresh smell of love making

Walking into grandma's....smell of fresh gingerbread

Charlie's home....smell of fresh cigar

Treating myself ....smell of new fresh leather

Trip to Spain .... fresh smell of open fire paella

Trip to Alabama...Friday night fresh fish fry smell

Stepping out of shower....fresh smell of clean

Just before surgery....fresh smell of hope

Believing scripture...fresh smell of promise

Falling in love....fresh smell of euphoria

Driving through a storm...fresh smell of victory

Pop a cork of prosecco...fresh smell of fizz

Pass driver's test @ 16...fresh smell of triumph

It's a boy/girl...fresh smell of miracles

Fresh

Inside Out—Outside In

There. Here.
Sunrise. Mid-day. Sunset.
Sand under, sky over, warm breeze
In between. Earth's sounds in surround-sound.
Neither Bose nor Audioengine can duplicate what
The ears hear live!
The ocean speaks, the wind embraces, the sky lifts, the horizon
Beckons. While I stand barefoot, my body is refreshed, my soul
Soothed, my spirit
Engaged while my eyes align with the horizon
Where earth meets sky, and I meet God
Ushered into His presence by the company and comfort of
The Holy Spirit.
Sunrise. Mid-day. Sunset.
Humming and singing from within – and nature harmonizes
From without. Inside out -outside in.
And la musica electronique via iphone.
All of nature, my body vocal wind instrument,
Powered by soul-spirit entwined
With instrumentals. Softly, loudly and somewhere in between.
And I need to dance in the infinite, undefined open spaces with
Reckless abandon. Singing in
Soft whispers and mind-blowing wind pipe maximum.
Inside-Out. Outside
In.

The Days of Seasons

Usually, I think of the seasons in four chunks of time
    Winter
    Spring
    Summer
    Fall

I never thought about thinking of the season in days, until

I heard "stretching across the 93 days of summer."

    Wow! Ninety-three days of summer, it no longer

Sounded endless, as we all fantasize. Poof goes

The fantasy (drum roll) and now enters reality. Disappointing,

Bubble bursting, "only" 93 days – not even 100?

Will we appreciate the first day and the last day more than

before? Then what of the 91 days in-between?

Enjoy the small talk chatter over dinner
    Stories and smores in back yard pits and beach fires

Make more home-made ice cream and
    Travel somewhere new

Summer still brings a sense of relief

    Time for fun, fun, fun...and more fun
    Outside – in the breeze
    in the sun

        in the rain

        in the dirt

        in the water

        in the sand

Between Raindrops

While I respect
       people are different
       I don't always
       understand and celebrate 'viva la difference'

Some folk dive in and become immersed in life – much
       like walking in the rain
       not bothered by getting
       caught in a downpour; and even
       enjoying the sensations of

feeling wetness on their face
       hearing the rush of the wind and rain
       seeing the dance of drops on the sidewalk
       tasting the refreshing droplets
       smelling the freshness of nature
       they don't try to walk between raindrops

Some simply appreciate a mild pitter-patter of
       raindrops in a gentle pattern of
       watered rhythm outside an open window
       they may wonder what's between raindrops

While others seek shelter by the 911
       umbrella, or a purse, or an
       attaché, or by the nearest
       awning or building
       wishing they were between raindrops

Then there are weather watchers who
       plan ahead and stay inside to

avoid any droplet contact

and never, ever ponder a raindrop, nor between raindrops

And then there are those who grumble

attempting a walk between the raindrops

missing the fun of

walking in

standing in

splashing in

sliding in

running in and simply

taking in the rain – drops

by walking between raindrops

The Bridge

Transitions are comparable to a bridge; but
Not tons of steel bridges with eight lanes
Envision a small, hand-crafted wooden bridge over a stream
In a quiet space—a tranquil place
Where one can listen and meditate

When the step is taken onto the unassuming bridge
Transition begins
The past seems more immediate, almost the present
And definitely more comfortable that the unknown future on the other
side

At times it might seem more comforting to step back–look back–hold on
to
What is familiar, even if painful, rather than walk into the mysterious
Half–way, standing there. Looking over the side, holding the curved rail
Feet unable, unwilling? to move.
STUCK

Let go of yesterdays and use the energy of today to move forward into
tomorrow
Let go of old baggage needing discard, occupying precious space needed
for
New thoughts, events, people, places, adventures, knowledge,
conclusions, ecstasies,
awards, escapades, disappointments

Ticks and Fleas

Dogs can have ticks and fleas
Lunch plates can have beans and peas
Butterfly wings can flutter and flip
Straws can be tools to gulp and sip

Grass blades can be green or brown
Hearing can have silence or sound
Water can be frozen or wet
Sun shines from dawn to sunset

Eyes can see open or closed
Women can be graceful tripped or posed
Children grow up by and by
Men are allowed to weep and cry

Life

Kiss the morning
Admire the sunset
Life is shorter than you think
Notice the clouds
Walk in the rain
Make a snow angel
Enjoy life, it keeps you sane
Take the trip
Make love spontaneously
Loose the weight
But still eat the candy, cookies, and cake
Slow to anger
Easy to love
Quick to listen
Slow to speak
Buy the shoes
Wear the dress
Say "I love you"-lots
Hug more
Laugh a lot
Cry when needed
Scream if you must
Forgive and forget
Embrace each day with gratitude
Close each evening with thanks
Be happy and
Do what makes you happy!

Defined

How are we defined by others?

Are we defined by the worse thing we have done
OR
by the best thing we have done?

Are we defined by the worst thing we have said
OR
by the best thing we have said?

Does it matter how others define us
OR
how we define ourselves?

New Kind of Rainbow

God's rainbow in the sky is magnificent to behold
Such a beautiful spectrum of colors
Arched stretching across His canvas from horizon to horizon
Is our view from earth looking <u>upward?</u>

Looking <u>downward</u> from 30,000 feet
The rainbow is not obscured by the horizon
It its full glory, it is circular
A never-ending symbol of His unbroken promise.

Alas, out of Africa comes a moving rainbow
A beautiful spectrum of color
Unheld hands across the sphere of earth's surface
100% cacao to milk chocolate to mocha to caramel to latte.

Out of Africa they have all come
Dispersed to other lands
Evolving over time to all melanin shades
To display a human rainbow.

Are violets blue?

Some roses 'are' red,
Are all violets shades of blue?
Besides the white ones, I see violets as purple-ly
And, so it is with love coming in many colors.
Not merely like a rose, beyond its many varieties,
The natural red, pink, white, yellow compounded
With man's enhancements, creating hybrids. Now,
Ain't that just like mankind? Can't appreciate what's
Already provided...wonderfully made in nature
From love? Nope, gotta try and make what is already
Perfection...into his ideal. Like space,
Outer space, that is. Earth with all of its resources
Wasn't appreciated, cherished, preserved. The
Solution? Outer space—other planets to inhabit.
I'm striving to see what I see before me—and appreciate
The varieties of rose-colored flowers; and the one true
Color of violets... in flowers and beyond... in
All things

Lotus

Fred said, you remind me of a lotus,
And so I was...reflecting over time.
Throughout my journey
I have emerged from
The weights of life. Upward and
Onward from the muck and mire of
Negative encounters and the daily
Grind. To survive on hope and possibilities
For focus and inspiration. Akin to the lotus
Drawn upward daily to fresh air, guided by
Gentle beams of light from the sun above
The water. Just like the water cleanses the
Lotus of muck and mire on the ascent, so did
Music soothe my Soul each morning; ritually
Emerging from life's blows. Day after day
The lotus re-emerges, unscathed; and
So have I. The lotus, the sun, the water and
Me created by God. The Son of the living God,
The Master of the sea–heard the despairing
Cries of my soul. And by the power of God's
Holy Spirit—He lifted me up—time and time
Again—from the water, from the water,
From the water He lifted me up...
Every time, often with angels, out of the muddy
Sediment of life. As the lotus rests atop the
Water; I rest in Him and find peace and solace.
Yours truly,
Lotus, aka Lotusness, Lotusious, Lotusiousness, Her Lotuship

Civility

Last night, as I lay sleeping
I ran into a dream, where
I was back in time, in
The motherland of mankind.
That's Africa. Then to other indigenous lands
Of those who migrated from Africa to
Native America and Asia. People were
Polite in discourse. Agreeing and disagreeing
Because they had a heightened commitment
To the virtues of civility. Then I fast forwarded
To current times, and time zones where public
Discourse seems archaic and under-developed
And under-evolved. Has the 1960's erosion of trust
For the establishment continued?
I awakened abruptly. The questions, unanswered:
Where are honesty and compromise?
Where are the virtues of civility?

Are You Listening

Sometimes the body whispers.
       Do we hear?
Sometimes the body calls out.
       Do we harken?
Even when the body yells.
       Do we listen?
For most—only when it finally screams in pain
       Do we pay attention!

Then are drastic measures needed, or
       Is it too late?

Are you listening to your body?
Are you listening to your soul?
Are you listening to your spirit?
No worries, time will tell.

Breathing Place

I've needed space to breathe
I feel like I'm in a place
Where I can breathe
On my own
No protection needed
Safe to be vulnerable
At will freedom
License to be free
In this space
My breathing place

Which Way is Up

Cellular...
intelligence
fortitude
metabolism
respiration
mutations
shapeshifting
data entry
data retrieval
resetting
reviving
restoring
remapping
refiring
oxygen
mitochondria
toxins
tapping
polarity
electricity
energy
parasites
nutrition
liver
stress
trauma
negative
positive

Cobwebs and Lint

Who can say where cobwebs come from?
Inside and outside in corners and ledges
Sometimes on rocks, often on hedges.

Cobwebs in our bodies are totally unseen.
Maybe interstitium is the thing
A wanna be organ of sorts to cling

Not to worry, a little exercise each day
Will swoosh all the cobwebs away.
Just work up a sweat, have fun, play.

As we get older, cobbies are a bore,
Cousins to bags, n sags, wrinkles and more.
Keeping up with all of it became a loathsome chore.

Multiple decades plus some years had passed
When I noticed cobs, the reality, the shock, I gasped
Webbies on my bosom and on my precious place
Too harsh, too startling truths to face.

When did all this happen? Why couldn't I see
Gradual cobwebs all over me?
First it was the hand, then the knees and chin.
Dear Lord, Lordy, Lawd! Will it never end?
And then there's lint!

Warm, Hot, Cold

What has changed in 55 years?
Then, his approach was inviting
Warmth in his eyes, his voice
So, I let him into my space, and what
Was experienced on my end was an unsure
Climate of seasonal shifts from warm, to hot, to
Cold. A revolving door. An illusion.
Unpredictable. Uncommitted. Inconsistent.
I moved on. Despite the good times
The good feelings—The budding of a love that
could have been L O N G.
Suddenly, four years ago, he connected indirectly.
Though he says my picture is before him, and
Daily he thinks of me, and loves me now, and
Always has. However, He seems stuck at the start of a race
And not moving. Skydiving without ever jumping.
Time ain't on our side, now in our mid-seventies
Which means staring at eighty. Yikes. Smile.
What's changed in 55 years? Not much.
I've been bold enough to be assertive—buuuuuut not
Aggressive. Expressing my interest.
When we chat and meet, it's all Warm. Then Cold.
Some like it warm, I guess some cold. Others like it hot. Whether young
or old.

Silence

Silence comes first, then the outer and inner noises.
For the first 18 weeks, the fetus exists in silence.
That translates to 4.139631 months, or 126 days, or 3024 hours.
In another 6 weeks, the little babe begins to distinguish sounds.
Hmmmmm.
Silence. So, let's see now. When can I recall hearing the
Sound of Silence? Not. Never.
Outer and Inner noises; inside and outside sounds; internal and external
timbres articulating
This and that – often repeating like echoes in a canyon, demanding
attention.
I made the choice to STOP! Quietly, yet firmly, I desired "silence" more
than familiar "sounds."
So, then, what is this unfamiliar Sound of Silence? Dunno. But wanna
know.

And so, it began.

Pause. Wait a sec. Before I could hear what I perceived to be no sound, I
had to
Figure - - - -out - - -how - - to - suspend my world.
The desire arose from within.
A soft demand for everything, the inner things and the outer things, to be
stilled,
Quieted. Ignored. To simply find
That before place. The 126 days place. The 3024 hours place of no
sound.

Is it at all Possible?

Is it still there? Beneath. Available? A needed resource? Why? Forgotten?
Retrievable?

Purpose? Would I need to recreate a womb-like mental state? Is it possible when

Asleep and/or awake?

A quiet spot – unfamiliar – on the floor – leaning on the soft, comfy corner of the gray wingback chair.

Sitting Waiting Choosing

To find my way back to silence. Eyes closed; ears commanded to focus. Shutting out the world

The greater challenge – quieting

My thoughts. Suddenly, I first saw blackness – a void – space – velvety and

Infinite...and then

An intense awareness of my ear canal – seemingly probing for the familiar.

Like a search light – scanning for any teenie detectable sound.

Willing to settle

For any! The most subtle. The rubbing of an ant's antenna; the flutter of a butterfly's wing; Or

The weaving of a spider's web. My choice for 'nothing' was superseding 'something'. Suddenly, the same velvet nothingness I

Saw – became what I heard. My ears stopped searching and just let me be Still. Peaceful. Almost serene. A pureness. Quieted to the sound of silence. Alas,

It felt vaguely familiar. From so long ago – those 126 days?

And now, my new awareness of Silence, No longer rare or unfamiliar. Now, a welcoming familiar practice. Sans noise inundation,

Just 2 minutes recharges the brain, boosts creativity, regulates heart and BP, invites mindfulness... .

The Reveal

People reveal who they are
One way or another
Sooner or later

Why do we ignore negative indicators?
When they tell us who they are
Why don't we believe them?

Is it because we are seekers of the good nature?
Is it because we want to believe in the best of the species?
Is it because we are in denial?

Sometimes it's obviously boldly present
No mystery, No hiding
Simply, "this is who I am"

Other times - it's subtle
Yes hidden, Yes delayed
Yes Disguised, Yes Veiled

Regardless of how or when, good or bad
When someone shows you who they are
Believe Them - The first time

JUST FOR FUN

7 Inches

Seven
S e v e n
1 2 3 4 5 6 7
Inches is an ipad mini
two lengthwise credit cards
standard size scissors
a #2 yellow pencil
2 crayons
4 golf balls
5 toothpicks
1 butter knife
10 dimes
Who decides what the inches will be?
Whether its 1, or 2, or 3
But why 7 inches, is a mystery.

New Goals

Aging into the 'seniors'
        brings new challenges
and new goals

Go on errands between 10:00am – 3:00pm
Place multiple pairs of glasses throughout home
Make it to the toilet dry
Walk back into the room for recall
Avoid rush hour interstate
Lock the front door
Keep notepad near – lists
Remember to look at the lists
        Have fun and don't set too many goals!

10,000

10,000 seconds is only 2 hours and 46 minutes

10,000 smiles take 10,000 seconds

10,000 kisses take many more seconds

10,000 peaches make 1,000 cobblers

10,000 infections make an epidemic

10,000 applauses request an encore

10,000 laces fit 5,000 pair of shoes

10,000 pencils write 5.5 billion alphabets

10,000 negative words change brain anatomy

10,000 kind words heal body soul spirit

10,000 snowflakes make a fantasy

10,000 soldiers make an army

10,000 fish feed a township

10,000 chickens lay 10,000 eggs in a day

10,000 raindrops equal ½ quart

10,000 wishes yields 10,000 dreams

Numbers are relative
10,000 may seem large from the low-end perspective
Or
10,000 can appear miniscule from the high-end
Is everything relative?

Something of Your Own

Having something of your own is
a solitary achievement
worth celebrating

What a boost to self-worth
identity
attitude
perspective

My something of my own
from an early age was
music
in my body
release in song

The core of my being
a wind-instrument
my soul sings
my spirit soars
my body exhales music

"I," and I alone control this
"I," and I alone give this freely
"I," and I alone can release this whenever I want

Every note on a 3½ octave range is
my gift
to me
to you to the world

And
I respond with joy and satisfaction
the world responds

Everyone needs something of their own
What's yours?

Boomers

Why are generations labeled and who decides?
The 'silent generation' before boomers had swingers and jitter buggers
and big bands
So how were they classified as
s i l e n t
and by whom?
Generations of cohorts, labeled and then what of it for
Gen X and Y and Z – opps! Y re-labeled 'millennials'
Do we become bound by the equities and inequities assigned?

Boomers may be the last of a breed
Newspaper readers and watching live TV
Cooking from scratch and reading books for leisure
Tasks that might give millennials a seizure

Boomers speak and text in whole sentences
And hold a conversation for more than five minutes
Boomers enjoy a sit-down family meal
The popular on-the-go-eating has little appeal

Boomers played board games when inside
Rode bikes, skated, and played outside
Their parents took leisurely evening walks
Or sat on porch swings having lively talks

Long gone are coffee clubs and fire-side radio
Ring washers, ice boxes, and gathering at a piano
Sneaking a cigarette or a sip of wine
Was as far as some committed a crime
Others on drugs and open sexuality
Brought new meaning to 'being free'

Balanced with responsibility
Boomers seem to have it all. Agree?

Wars and civil unrest
Repeated Gen challenges,
Not sure we passed the test
Now in seventies and eighties
Will they soon be put to rest?

Songs of the fifties and sixties ring clear
Many with ear devices help them hear
Melodies and lyrics in their memories live on
But soon Gens will be asking, where have all the boomers gone?

Apps

The "App" is here to stay
as electronic computing
Used to be a paper document
called an application
completed with a pen
typically to apply for a job
or college admissions
now referred to as "apps"
Is paper still a thing? Pen?
Did you download the app?
Oh, there's an app for that.
No more grocer paper coupons
Oh, there's an app for that.

Can I co-pay at my appointment?
No, we have an app for payments
            and "talking with the office"
Can I order delivery?
Oh, we have an app for that.

How far reaching will app technology go?
Maybe labor & delivery will have one tomorrow!

Down & Out?

Au contraire
Life has its punches.
Down, but
.........Not........... out!
Never.
Like 'Bobo the Clown'
Plastic air-filled toy with
Sand in the bottom
Bouncing
Back, punch
After punch. Like
A cat with nine lives,
Surviving the dips and dives.
Even close to death is
A life-altering encounter, seems
Surreal, nothing profounder. Or
Returning from the light or
The tunnel, or heaven, which
Is embodied in the number seven.
Attitude and choice must
Kick in every time you're down,
To bring you back on ground,
Once again, safe and sound.

Abstract and Concrete

Some things
Are difficult to put
Into words. Is it easier,
Or harder to define,
Or think in the realm of concrete
Or abstract?
Is it a strain to think in
Shapes
Colors
Sounds?
What is the shape, then of
Water
Fire
Wind
Dirt?
What is the color of
Air
Love
Tenderness
Fear?
What is the sound of
Silence
Red
Silk
Darkness?
And how would you think on these things in the concrete and in the
abstract?
Eye-rain Heart-ache Soul-joy Mental-ecstasy Sun-glare Body-pain
Spiritual-prayer
Total-climax Soft-weeping Sorrowful-grief Wedding-vows Newborn-
babe

Nene (nee-nee) Sugar Grandma

When the first grand baby was born
I thought, "she is as sweet as sugar."
I called her my sugar-baby.
When she was babbling, she
Converted grand-mommie to
Nene—and so I was forever
Nene, and I adored it.
With each new grand, the nest of
Sugar babies grew.
Twenty-seven years later, a friend
Referred to me as Sugar Grandma.
Now I have a first, middle, and last
Name: Nene Sugar Grandma

Auto Correct *#@%$

A.I. (artificial intelligence) versus H.I. (human intelligence) has become a personal issue.

Autocorrect on my cell phone is more annoying than robotic customer service.

A step forward in technology, auto correct, a form of A.I. overrides H.I. – human side. Human choice.

I am hearing more and more frustration from other seniors, of what I experience.

Were people always this impatient?

They act like autocorrect...

      Substituting your words

Finishing your sentences

Auto correct on my cell is one thing; however, 'human correct' is more difficult to manage.

Did they know I had a stroke? Doubt it.

Can they see my gray hair and facial lines? Perhaps.

The human side of autocorrect is worse than the artificial. *#@%$

The Collective Priority

Our
We
Us
Mine
Me
I

Three Sister Cousins

Susan, Kathryn, and Bonnyeclaire
Three little cousins, sitting in a chair
Three little cousins just meeting there
From the Miller tree 2 generations ago
They descended from 3 sisters; wouldn't ya know:

Kathryn from Maude Louise, first born, pretty as you please. Her beauty I am told was like a magnet for young and old. On a train to Alabama going faster and faster, after a brief stop it came to a near disaster. A man tried to steal her as a child. Made her mama, Ella, go plum wild. He was caught with her walking down the track. Her Daddy woulda given that man a smack.

Bonnyeclaire from Beatrice Vivian, 2nd born to Maude. A melodious singing voice deserving grand applause. Like her sister Maude, she was a teacher. Her husband Percy, a deacon, was close to the preacher. She didn't teach long and she lost her song when her house caught on fire, and Byron's death took her desire. She lived only one year after Maude. Died in 1928. Too young for her daughters, their lives never got straight.

And there's Susan from Emma Grace who loved the finer things like Italian lace. Baby girl of eleven, got whatever she wanted - like living in heaven. Full of life and charm, was easy to have a gentleman on her arm. Rode life like she rode horses, free and designing her own courses. Drove life like she drove a car, big and fine like the queen of a czar. She loved her mom and she loved her dad, all loved the two sons she had.

One thing in common had each sister girl, was a quest for life and giving life a whirl. Seems to be a trait of all Miller women. Great zest in life, even when the light of life was dimmin'. Beauty, intelligence, style and charm are surely passed down from their hearts so warm - through sons and daughters to find their way into the next generations until this very day.

Now, sit three cousins having a lively chat, about a family of members like braiding a plait. The first meeting was warm like their grandmother's lives were passing a baton to help the memories thrive. These three cousins now have a story to tell. How they met in Duluth GA and that it went well. No pictures are attached so imagine what you see, three cousins of three sisters came to meet.

Recipe

The recipe for getting along in life is uncomplicated

Be easy to love
Be quick to forgive
Haste to be kind
Slow to anger
Love unconditionally
Oh—and... be easy to love!

Dire Circumstances

It's not right
But it's real

When most fragile
I gained the most strength

From deep inside
Unknown before

Dire circumstances
Opened a secret door

SOME

Some ideas take longer to form
Some facts take longer to prove
Some research takes longer to find
Some pages take longer to turn
Some thoughts take longer to write
Some chapters take longer to read
Some fish take longer to fry
Some minds take longer to harden
Some hearts take longer to forgive

Some people come for a fleeting moment
Some come for a few hours, sharing a seat on a train
Some come for a night, like a ride across the sky on red-eye
Some come for season, we may or may not know the reason
Some come for a life-time, which can have all manner of impact

Some crumbs are harder to grasp
Some rain drop wetness seems to last
Some heat-of-the moment is just that
Some acts of kindness resonate a lifetime
Some spilt milk does make us cry
Some of anything good is better than nothing

Some

Covid Loco

Did I actually go there? Or
Is it all in my mind?
Is this Covid Loco?

Did I really say that to someone? Or
Was it to myself?
Is this Covid Loco?

Like a worn-out refrain
I'm sheltered, sheltered, sheltered in
Place, place place
Goggles over my eyes
Mask on my face, face face.
Is this Covid Loco?

Shield of plastic strapped to my head
Cotton in my ears
Rubber gloves in colors-no red
Is this Covid loco?

Can't sleep at night
No peace in the day
How much longer can I go on
This way?
This is Covid Loco!!!!!!!

The Instrument

Ohhhh. You think it's easy to sing
Maybe so—Maybe not.
Using the human body—the whole of it
Is an awesome concept as a vocal instrument

It is not the same as talking, or whispering, or shouting

Far beyond the basics of melody and lyrics
There is relationship
With one's self
With the composer, the lyrist
With the listener(s)

There is a surrender to the notes, and
The space between each note
A flow and ownership of sound and
Rhythm in time and sequence and
The space before and after the upbeats and downbeats

While discovering one's own interpretation inwardly
To project outwardly, connecting to the listeners, the
Words and meaning, and emotion, the story
Set to melody, in frequencies converted to energy
Which become invisible light—rainbow rays of something universal

The instrument of the human voice is most powerful when the vocalist
totally surrenders
Entering a zone, becoming one with the music and words and tone

KA

KA was classified "a pretty Negro girl."
Hazel eyes, fair skin. Little thick in the thighs for a dancer
She didn't date brothas ????
Not even Ivy Lea-gueas
To her they were all neegas

She wanted the other boys
Privileged, smart, and rich
The problem—they didn't see eye to eye
Couldn't get past her kin
Couldn't get past her skin

She died young-er than one would expect
So sad, an only child with much potential
Never married, labeled an old maid
Could have had a jack of spades.

PERSPECTIVES

What is the difference between a mistress
and
 a whore?
Oh noooo! Did you really open that door?

What is the difference between a pimp
and
a madam?
Maybe only about the size of a badam.

What's the difference between a drug dealer
and
greedy prescription writer?
One's a dealer and one's a healer.

What's the difference between a drape
and
a curtain?
Fancy and plain, of that I am certain.

What's the difference between a carton
and
a box?
Carton is thin, box strong as an ox.

What's the difference between you
and
me?
I'm looking at you through my words
And you're looking back at me!

SIMPLY DIVINE

Dying

What is the experience of dying and death?
There is a list of sayings...
Parting is sweet sorrow
I'm so sorry for your loss
Please accept my sincerest condolences
Too young to leave so soon
Lived a full life
In a better place
...and the list goes on.

There are beliefs...
No life after death
Life after death
A place called hell
A place called heaven
Reincarnation
No reincarnation.

The transition, some say is
A bright light that guides you
Angels come to escort you
Nothing, that's the end of existence
Perhaps what comforts is a simple explanation that any person, age, or
culture can understand.

Death is not the end. It is like walking into the next room with new
experiences and challenges.
You take who you are, the memories, and emotions with you.
You are near so the ones you leave on the other side of the door remain
close.
It's a continuum...time is infinite...a seamless flow of previous, current,
and future existence.

How

the day is yet young
    full of energy and possibility and
    openness to whatever
    serendipitous moment that may present
    there is time for everything and
    everyone – breathe and pace
    in the space of the place where you are
    for the body, soul, and spirit are best
    when the internal systems are at rest
and the night is patient
    quickly surrendering to
    the clock of peace and
    rest of a different kind
    giving grace to tasks and thoughts
    left behind for another day –
    replay, but for now pause
it will all get done under the
    light and warmth of another sun
    then the morning
    comes in a new dawn, overlooking
    all that transpired since
    the dimming dusk, bringing again
a day that is young and a night that is patient

The Miracle

What is so special...so unique about a miracle?
I'm sitting in Charles De Gaulle Aéroport.

I'm hearing French, so why am I not thinking in French?
Arrived in Spain, so why not thoughts in Spanish?

Poorly prepped, my native tongue is my only one, except
The smidgen of several languages I learned as a
mezzo soprano like tapas in French, German, Spanish, Italian,
 and Latin seem to have faded.

I'm hopeful, even with the passage of time and
the gray matter damage from Stachybotrys chartarum
and the brain clot, there is a reservoir of some
basic know how...would that qualify as a miracle?

I have experienced miracles—and some events of surprise
that resemble miracles. I am now in the midst of
or in the realm of a miracle.
I had a desire. I expressed the desire.

And then, without further effort on my part
 – it happened. A miracle was bestowed upon me,
initiated by another being other than myself?
Was this a God-sent miracle? Was it a man-made miracle?

Or was it the power of the spoken tongue creating miracles
by eliciting from heaven or from earth or both?
I had an ailment. I prayed. A solution came to me.
I followed the instructions. The ailment was remedied.

'That' was a miracle...no human explanation for it. Defies logic?
What is so special about a miracle is when

you witness one, directly or indirectly. And that a
miracle is original and personal makes it unique!

All over the world
Miraculum Latin, Miracle old French, Meidan Greek,
Smejo ("to laugh" old church) Skavonic,
Milagro Spanish, Miracolo Italian, Wonderwerk Afrikaans. Chozizwa
Chichewa, Mu'ujiza Hausa, Milagre Portugese,
Ora ebube Yorbu, Mujiso Somali, Miujiza Swahili,
Iyanu Yoruba, Ngesimangaliso Zulu, Miracle English.

Music

Music is the language of God
Music is His breath
Music brings us closer to God than anything
Whole heart in it

Singing converts the body into a woodwind instrument
Singing "Hallelujah" is the highest form of sung praise/worship – Halal
Dance – movement of the parts makes its own music
Instruments, like singing and dancing use the brain and the body
Whole body in it

Music is liberating, soothing, inspiring, energizing, healing
Music has the ability to carry our souls to a time, place, emotion, thought
Music can create and enhance imaginations
Whole mind in it

Music is an opportunity for spiritual elevation
Music invites the anointing of the Holy Spirit
Music transcends earthly presence
Whole spirit in it

The Infilling

Come my beloved.
I desire to move in your heart.
The Spirit of the Lord comes as an exhorter
Speaking as the mouthpiece of the Father
In this hour.

Daughters, you are lovely as a rose and the lily.
Your inner beauty creates a fragrance only I can smell.
Sons, you are handsome like the oak and the muscadine.
Mighty men of valor with an odor only for my nostrils.
Mark 10:9 is often misunderstood, limiting it to earthly marriages
However, there is a deeper meaning – a greater spiritual parallel in
"Whatever God hath joined together, let not man put asunder."
This is parallel to the bride and the bridegroom and the bridechamber as
in
Mark 25:1 "The kingdom of heaven is likened to 10 virgins," both female
and male.
Father desires to fill your vessels with oil so that you, as the lamp, not only
shine
Your light on earth – but to enable you stay joined with Him AND
Avoid the subtleties of spiritual adultery – And be prepared to enter into
the
Bridegroom chamber.

Seek me now, if you desire to be filled. Not just a portion, but FILLED.
Surrender, and let
The Holy Spirit first trim your lamp (purge you) for in trimming the
wick, oil from your reservoir, which is
the Holy Spirit, can be drawn up into you... so that your
Flame is clean and bright – as is that of the Holy Spirit.
Come my beloved.

Time

Time to wait

        Time to heal

        Time to work

        Time to play

        Time to speak

        Time to listen

        Time to run

        Time to rest

        Time to love

Time to care

        Time to pray

        Time to be

Time to sing

        Time to dance

        Time to laugh

        Time to cry

        Time to know

        Time to ask

        Time to hug

        Time to kiss

Time for everything, nothing to miss
What we need time for, we have time for. Time.

The Question

Faith shaken
Worry crowding
Doubt creeping
Tears flowing
My question. Have you heard my prayer? My anguish is greatly pressing
upon me
His question: Have I ever failed you? I am Emanuel.
Not only has God never failed me—He has always been faithful. He is
Faith.
When my heart had no song
When my heart turned away from Him
When my heart was breaking
When my heart was lost
When my heart was dark
When my heart was empty
When my heart was shattered
When my heart was hateful
When my heart was angry
When my heart had envy
When my heart was lonely
When my heart had no song
When the lyrics were gone
I lost the melody of life
Because my spirit was broken
Love in my soul was lost
My body could not produce a melody
by the loss of joy and hope,
By life's crushing blows.
Through it all God has been faithful, to rescue me

Tetelestai

T E T E L E S T A I ? Tetelestai, indeed.
Ummmmm.....Greek.......perfect tense......no English equivalent
Past tense
      Present tense
      Future tense
All wrapped up in one single word.

Soooooooooo.....the word is fluid....continuous.....no time barrier
Past flows into
      Present flows into
      Future flows into
Infinity....forever....everlasting results
How utterly amazing and beautiful and awesome!

Therefore, in the final hour when
"Tetelestai" was uttered, the past was completed in the present for all
time to come.
It is finished...indeed.

I wish English had perfect tense.
      Maybe I will learn Greek (a little).

Declaration

The Lord God Almighty reigns
The blood of Jesus flows thru my veins
The anointing of God is in me
The devil can only deceive me

Be a woke believer
Of His word a receiver
Believe, receive victorious
A witness, testimony glorious

Got forgiveness at the cross
Got salvation at the cross
Got healing at the cross
Got provision at the cross

Healthy food feeds my body
Holy word feeds my soul
Healing scripture is medicine
Let the truth now be told

Live with love, not fear
The Lord is always near
Live with joy, not sorrow
Chose life today and tomorrow

Live free from sin
Open your heart
Open your mind
Let the anointing come in

Two Sides of Hell

Two sides of a living hell is
  being a woman in a man's world
  being Black in a White world
  being a Black woman in a White man's world

Two sides of a living hell is
  being too brown to be White
  and too light to be Black
  then being judged by both

Two sides of a living hell is
  expecting Whites to give you hell
  but not anticipating Blacks as well
  to give you two sides of a living hell

Were You There?

Part 1 Inquiry as the Prelude

The first healing remembrance and tribute to my three friends of the four girls in the Sixteenth Street Church bombing: Cynthia, Denise, and Carol

September 15, 1963

Part 1, 2003, 40 years after the incident

Inquiry

Were you there on September Sunday morn?
Were you there on September Sunday morn?
Ohhhhh, sometimes it causes me to tremble, tremble, tremble
Were you there on September Sunday morn?

4 young girls were gathered, to wash their hands
When bombs struck at the hand of evil men
Oh ohhhh ohhh sometimes it causes me to tremble, Tremble, TRE-EH-EM-BLE
Were you there when they came to the house of God?

Were You There

Part 2 Tribute, the continuation

The healing finally resolved after 50 years. To my three friends, of the four girls, in the Sixteenth Street Church bombing:

Cynthia, Denise, and Carol - September 15, 1963

Prelude (Part I - 2003) 40 years after 1963

Were you there on September Sunday morn?

Were you there on September Sunday morn?

Ohhhhh, sometimes it causes me to tremble, tremble, tremble

Were you there on September Sunday morn?

4 young girls were gathered, to wash their hands

When bombs struck at the hand of evil men

Oh ohhhh ohhh sometimes it causes me to tremble, Tremble, TRE-EH-EM-BLE

Were you there when they came to the house of God?

Tribute (Part 2 - 2013) 50 years afterwards

Were you there when they sacrificed 4 lives?

Did you hear 4 innocent girls have died?

Ohhhh ohhh sometimes it causes me to tremble, tremble, tremble

Were you there when they sacrificed 4 lives?

All over town we heard the blasted bomb

It shook the world, and carved a lasting tomb

Sometimes it causes me to wonder, wonder, wonder

All over town we heard the blasted bomb.

Stunned and shocked in total disbelief

Bruised hearts pumped blue, and black in saddened grief

Sometimes it causes me to ponder, ponder, ponder

Stunned and shocked in total disbelief.

118

Families moaned and walked the trail of tears
Tears they have shed, for all these fifty years
Sometimes it causes me to crumble, crumble, crumble
To recall of death of my sweet peers.

Freedom rings a little louder now
A job well done, their legacy is how
Sometimes it causes me to wonder, wonder, wonder
How these girls sped up the freedom plow.

Just one year later in 1964
Civil Rights was passed on the Senate floor
Sometimes it causes me to ponder, ponder, ponder
Your sacrifice closed segregation's door.

Although the struggle continuous on
Your flame is brighter since you've been gone
Sometimes it causes me to tremble, tremble, tremble
To recognize the seeds your lives have sown.

Ohhhh oh ohhhhh sometimes it causes me to
            tremble, Tremble, T R E M B L E
Deaths not in vain, your legacy of forgiveness lives on

You Are

Popular, popular is "you are what you eat"
and you are how you exercise and sleep!
Blah, blah blah – but is that all that you are?
a walking container of air and energy
wrapped in a system of internal synergy?

Is that all you are? Nope, you are ⅓ body
and the world cannot agree
what exacting is the rest of you and me

Welp! There's the soul containing mind and heart
that's another third; however, at the start
the spirit was there mysteriously extant
So that's three thirds, what do you think?

We cannot just be, blah blah blah, only what we eat
Out of the heart and mind, maybe we are what we think
Or
What we feel or what we do
What of this is theory and what is true?

Maybe, just maybe we are what we believe
Could belief drive everything we conceive?
One thing is for sure
we are more than what we eat
three thirds of body soul and spirit
makes us complete

The Ultimate Loss

The phone rang
My heart sank
Premature labor
Five months in
Lungs too fragile
No options on the table
Except abort or give birth

Choosing the latter
Made night turn to day
Waiting and praying
As I tried to stay awake
The moment came
And fleeting it was
She took one breath
The thought left me hollow

The dream of grandbaby love
Which is the greatest love of all
When loss, sucks the air out
As you feel yourself fall
Into a dark pit of despair
For grand # seven
Was now gone, up in heaven

We had done prissy shopping
My daughters and me
And I had visions of
Dressing her and combing her hair
Rocking while singing her to sleep
All disappeared with no replacements

I traveled a thousand miles and while on the plane
I wrote eleven pages expressing my pain
When I looked into her parent's eyes
The same darkness I felt, stared back in sorrow
I had to find strength to comfort and give faith
Though on shaky ground, somehow, the family found grace

Contemplation and prayer gave me hope
The music of Andre Bocelli gave me peace
I played the CD for a solid year
The only consolation that soothed my ache
Comforting melody with time, healed my heart
With her warm tender memory, her face—precious art.

Plight

The single mom's plight
Can be fight or flight
If she does not discern
Of what to let go and learn
Stressors daily need to be dismissed
Even though demands persist

After the devastation of divorce
She is left to find her course
Navigating every second of every minute of every hour of every day
She must make all decisions that come her way

Children's needs, like birdlings in a nest
Dictate her schedule, on demand, with little rest
Answered prayers from God above
Carry her through with heavenly sent love

Angels appeared when the car didn't start
Kind neighbors and friends uplift her heart
Money appeared once in a bush, then on the ground
Abundant blessings pouring – miracles abound

Ahhhhh,
At last she learns how to lighten the load
Staying at rest, in a God trusting mode

Daisies and God

When I was young, younger
As a little girl, and as a blossoming teen
Countless hours were spent choosing
Just the right daisy.
Once chosen, to gently pluck it from its nourishing
Anchor and sit comfortably to inquire
With a boy in mind, or not
To ask the famous repetition
"He loves me, he loves me not"
Banking, if desired that the final
Petal, would lastly be the former
And of course, the latter if he was yuckie!
What about God?
Every petal, like the girlish ritualized rhyme
Repeats
However, it's a different rhyme
He loves me, he loves me still
Sublime
And
Real

Blame God

When we need to blame somebody when things go
Wrong in life – Why not blame God? Many people do.
But wait? Why? Is that an easy cop out?
Is God the only influencer?
Are there other considerations for impact?
What about decisions and choices we make?
Consider the cause and effect of other's actions?
Evil spiritual forces?
Opposing natural laws like gravity?
Free will?
Seems like free will and making counter choices is what
Started things going sideways, upside down, and backwards
From the beginning. One rule, broken.
Things go wacky...just blame God?
Disregard causes of unwanted consequences?
And just...well...you know- blame Him.
Cut corners on manufacturer's guidelines, and something
Goes wrong? Put regular gas in a diesel engine? Or
Water or OJ. Oops!
Go against nature and see what happens. Jump off
A cliff or the roof of a building and see if
Gravity won't plummet you to injury or death.
Still blaming God?
He does not need defending—this is merely a commentary on
Observations of peoples' reactions to hardships,
Mishaps, and miseries. Sometimes, even mere inconveniences.
Many use the easy way out seeking a scapegoat. And
That is usually to simply... blame God.

Sad Eyes

Explanation: This poem was written, in part, after looking at the pics on the one-hour PBS Slave Narratives link sent to me by Marion G. (2013); and it was completed after reading many 1930's recorded WPA Virginia slave narratives assigned by Dr. Patterson in Oral History (2014). While not all slaves' eyes were sad, too many were. The words of Frederick Douglass echo the sentiment: "the cheerful spark that lingered about my eye died; the dark night of slavery closed in upon me." If eyes are the window to the soul, then they may be considered reflections of bondage, and of the suffering endured by continuous seasoning tactics. This poem was written during a six-month period, 2013-2014, in MA studies.

Sad Eyes

two eyes, sad eyes.
you eba seed de eyes ob de slave?
dey roun like uhra eyes an set square in de head
like uhra eyes. de be peekin an lookin an gazin
an poppin n sobbin n cryin jes like uhra folk eyes,
cept dey don't be lightin an gleamin an flittin an
flurtin an smilin like dem uhras.
round, preetie brown eyes
beautiful. beautiful dark brown eyes.
dough some be light brown, o' hazul,
o' green, o' eben blue – dey moslie
be dark coffee bean brown.
you evah seed eyes ob de slave?
dey be sad eyes
sadlyest two eyes on earf.
slave eyes is quiet eyes – moslie,
cept when dey weeps an sobs an cries.
But moslie dey be silent crys of silent eyes.
you evah seed slave eyes?
dey is de eyes what been beat
dey is de eyes what been whup
dey is de eyes what been stole
dey is de eyes what been sold
dey is de eyes what been starved
dey is de eyes what been crushed
dey is de eyes what been kilt
dey is de eyes what be wilt
dey is the eyes what been robbed
robbed o' de joy o' life
so the light gone.

dey is dark
dey is sad,
mos' nearly all dey hope
done
sho
nuff
gone....
gone when dey left mother land
cross da big wata.
gone when sold dey mama an
dey mama churen.
gone when sold dey papa and
dey papa churen
all dey peoples whar dey be...
bout nearly gone... an some fo ehba gone.
you ehbar seed slave eyes?
slave eyes is watchful eyes
mos' like dey eyelibs is ears.
watchin and listenin fo whn
white skin com ta suck black skin.
sometime be da misses sending fo jo-jo
cause he young strong eye candy.
mosta time be a sista gotta do what massuh
n any o kinda sweated white skin wanna.
even sneaking be de misses
wan de chocolate sista
o' massuh wan jo-jo.
uh-huh chille.
sad eyes be seein and listenin eyes
but moslie, dey be sad eyes.
sad eyes is slave eyes
an slave eyes is sad eyes,

pitiful-sorrowful-painful
  kusikitisha macho,

  yeux tristes,

  indhaha murugo,

  mwute anya,

  bà oju,

  m idanu,

  amehlo sad,

  hartseer oë *

  sad eyes

uh-uh, no suh, don't madda what color YOU is,

deh be in all pretty black, Black uhns sho as dey be wit massa's lite uhns,

chile, you eba seed dem slave eyes?

i is—i jes seed em ta day, I be sees em eba day

sho nuff—dem slave eyes sad, sad eyes

cause dem slave eyes be de eyes ob de seasoning

what ain neba stop...

ain

neba

stop.

* "Sad eyes" translation is respectively listed in Kiswahili, Krio, Somali, Igbo, Yoruba, Hausa, Zulu, Afrikaans. No translation available for Wolof, Twi, Tigrinya, and Setswana. I have been advised that the word 'sad' does not exist in the Setswana language.

Let

Yes. That is the title. L E T
Such a small word.
So unassuming.
Does anyone notice "let" at any time?
At the beginning of a sentence?
The middle or the end of a phrase?

Even when God spoke it in Genesis,
Who noticed "let"?

Oh of course there was
The Light and the Dark
The Sun and the Stars
The Valleys and Mountains
The Waters and the Land
And the Man and the Woman

None of it would have occurred without "LET"
So, now, pause, and rethink it.
Focus on the "power of let."

About the Author

Bonnyeclaire Smith Stewart is a versatile storyteller, using her talents in writing, song, dance, drama, and more since childhood. Her first public poetry recitation, as kindergarten class poet, was at age five. Her book, "Become the Pebble," draws on her life experiences from Birmingham, Alabama to international travels. Bonnyeclaire has found poetic expression to be both an anchor and a release in her personal and professional life. She has served in leadership roles in non-profit and business sectors, having earned an MA and an MBA. This book of poems brings the comfort of the familiar, with her fresh perspective on shared human experiences.

To learn more about Stewart and the organization she founded - 4MillionVoices—visit: 4MillionVoices.com

Acknowledgements

I first acknowledge life given to me by God through my parents; and all those who have crossed my path for a moment, a season, or a lifetime. I thank my children–Adrienne, James, and Lisa– and infinite generations of ancestors in family and community who came before me. I am especially grateful to poetic women of color whose words imparted insights, strength, and connectedness beginning with Phyliss Wheatley to the present-day Amanda Gorman.

While my heart would engage a long list of life influencers, these next mentions are those who I acknowledge for influencing my writing:

Carol Lewis Thompson, former editor of Current History Magazine, aka "Aunt Carol," and Clifford, "Cliff" Barton, as dedicated family friends, were masters of the English language who tutored me in written expression, and editing during my high school years.

Professor Joseph Campbell, PhD, for planting the 'follow your bliss' seed in 1968 at Sarah Lawrence College during the first semester of my senior year. This introspective process of discovering and staying mindful of moments when you are happiest can lead to a life of fulfillment if one remains in that flow state. Self-observation of the coherence of heart and mind in your happiest moments can lead to self-actualization by engaging in activities that keep you in the flow of happiness. He understood the connection between poets and this introspective process. He described poets as the most attentive listeners of bliss language: "poets are simply those who have made a profession and have a lifestyle of being in touch with their bliss." It took many years for me to understand Campbell's theory. Out of that birthed the notion that to shift from the state of being into the state of doing, one must become the pebble to truly follow your bliss.

Diana Chambers Leslie, for inviting me to her weekly meditation and poetry group; and gifting me with Em Claire's poems, "Home Remembers Me." Inspired, I revisited several journals and casually filed poems written on loose papers, napkins, index cards, and various other surfaces that held my thoughts and feelings transferred by pen and pencil. And for whom I am grateful for writing the foreword.

Bernadette Noll, whose entire poem "Sea Glass" expresses sentiments that resonate deeply within my soul, beginning with the opening: "I want to age like sea glass, smoothed by time, but not broken."

Specific defining moments include:

Dr. Aubry Gardner, who said, "You are a scholar and you have much to say."

Dr. Stephanie Evans, Graduate Department Chair, whose initial interaction conveyed, "I see you. You matter. This is a place where you can develop your research ideas."

Dr. Kathryn W. Takara, who encouraged me to write in all manner of written expression. I appreciate her seasoned perspective as a publisher and author in her review of this collection of poems.

Other Published Works by Author

Essay: "Hypocrisy in the Life of W.E.B. DuBois: Reconstructing Selective Memory"
Phylon, Vol 51, No 1, Fall 2014, pp 57-75 Clark Atlanta University
Stable
http://www.jstor.org/stable/43199121
https://www.coursehero.com/file/39463171/RP-Hypocrisy-in-the-Life-of-WEB-Du-Bois-Reconstruting-Selective-Memorypdf/

Interview: "About George Griffin, Hartford CT butler of Mark Twain"
Mark Twain Journal, Vol 53, No 1, Spring 2015, pp 114-121
https://www.jstor.org > stable > i24612772
https://www.jstor.org > stable > 24612782

Master's Theses: "Front Doors-Back Doors: Hypocrisy of Mark Twain Towards His Servants"
Robert W. Woodruff Library, Atlanta University Center
https://dlg.usg.edu/record/auu_cau-td_2015-smith-stewart-bonnyeclaire
http://hdl.handle.net/20.500.12322/cau.td:2015_smith_stewart_bonnyeclaire
https://radar.auctr.edu/islandora/object/cau.td%3A2015_smith_stewart_bonnyeclaire

www.ingramcontent.com/pod-product-compliance
Lightning Source LLC
LaVergne TN
LVHW041225080426
835508LV00011B/1079